I have been working as software engineer professional in a multinational firm for more than 20 years. I feel its time to leverage my learnings over the years and mentor programmers on practices of writing reliable, maintainable and extensible software. I have learned lot of good coding practices the hard way by making mistakes first and learning from them along the way. Design patterns have helped me tremendously to avoid repeating those mistakes. This book documents commonly used creational design patterns and attempts to provide guidelines on how to avoid common pitfalls on software development by using right design patterns.

A Mckinsy study of 5,400 large scale IT projects (projects with initial budgets greater than $15M) in 2012 reported that 17 percent of large IT projects go so badly that they can threaten the very existence of the   company. It also mentioned that on average, large IT projects run 45 percent over budget and 7 percent over time, while delivering 56 percent less value than predicted. A lot of these problems can be attributed to bad code that becomes unmaintainable as code size grows. The Pareto principle indicates that 80 percent of outcomes can be attributed to 20 percent of the possible causes of a given event. Also known as the 80-20 rule, it's relevant to almost every field of human endeavor. The principle also applies to software engineering by saying that most problems are caused by a small number of bad coding practices. These practices can be eliminated by using design patterns thereby helping engineers and companies become more productive and successful.

Design patterns offer proven solutions to commonly recurring problems. When you see a common recurring problem, you find a common, general solution to solve it. It happens in architecture, mechanics, usability, and human behavior, and programming makes no exception.   These solutions have been tried successfully in the past. This book attempts to bring awareness of these successful patterns among developer community.

I was impressed by Gang of Four's design patterns early on. I have used design patterns in large projects and was astounded by the amount of reusability the code offers when it makes use of right design pattern.   Having knowledge design patterns creates a high level of maturity. Armed with knowledge, developer can look at bigger picture and thinks about extensibility and reusability before jumping into doing.   Design patterns also happens to be one of favorite topics among interviews for software engineer. Hence having design pattern knowledge will give you an edge. It will take you to journey of becoming ninja developer.

This book covers creational design patters, Creation pattern enables programmer to build solutions to writing code that creates object(s) in fashion that keeps code extensible, maintainable and reusable.

Introduction

Design Patterns provide easy to recognize and use OOP solutions to common problems. They're inherently easy to maintain, because many people are familiar with them. This is very similar to how google works. Everyone knows HOW to google, so when you get a query like "What is the purpose of design patterns", you can very quickly use this common interface to solve a problem.

Design pattern can greatly increase efficiency, reliability and productivity of developer team as whole as it offers proven and tested solutions.

Creational design patterns are all about various ways in which class can be instantiated. The instantiation method varies based on what and how much of it developer want to control from consumer of code. This pattern is classified int class-creation patterns and object-creational patterns. While class-creation patterns use inheritance effectively in the instantiation process, object-creation patterns use delegation effectively to get the job done. This gives your program more control in deciding which objects need to be instantiated for a specified use case.

In Java, the way to create an object is to use **new** operator.

Foo = new Foo() ; // Instance of Foo class

Let us say it's you who has written Foo class and gave the library to someone to use it. As you can see, the user of this library can instantiate any number of Foo classes with absolutely no control. Also here we are hard coding the way object is getting instantiated. In many cases, exact object that needs to be created depends on runtime behavior. Creation design patterns abstract the way object can be created. It can make program more flexible and generic.

- Factory Method
  It provides a class that decides what object need to be instantiated from a family of classes that are derived from common abstract class based on input data provides.
- Abstract Factory
  It provides ability to create instance of several families of classes
- Builder
  It provides ability to differentiate object construction from its representation. Hence depending on the need , various representations can be created.
- Prototype
  It provides lightweight method of creating new objects by cloning or copying existing instances.
- Singleton
  It provides ability to control number of instances that can be created by restricting it to one instance.

CHAPTER ONE

Factory

Background

Factory design patterns are useful in scenario where there is need to create instance of a class from related family of classes. For instance say there is a factory that makes electronic toys. All electronic toys share some common characteristic like they have a play and stop button. If you need a teddy bear, all you need to tell to factory is "Hey make me teddy bear" and the factory will make one for you and give it back to you.

If you need a tiger, you need to tell to factory is "Hey make me a tiger" and the factory will make tiger and give it back to you. In this case the user just passes in description of toy and let factory create the toy for user. The use can press play and stop button on the toy after purchasing the toy. Same factory can create other electronic toys like lion, dog etc. based on user need.

Implementation

Usually all of the classes have parent class and common functions. But each function operates on task differently. In addition there is a factory class that handles responsibility of understanding what class user needs, instantiating the required class and returning that instance. In the electronics toy factory example, all toys have common function called play, and each toy plays differently. When a teddy bear is asked play, it may sing a song. When tiger is asked to play, it may emit roaring sound. This relationship is explained in picture below.

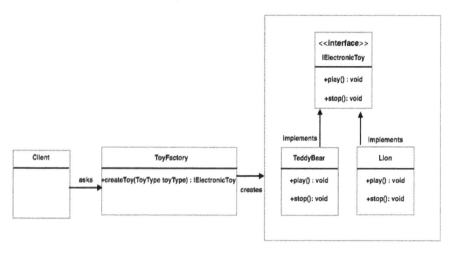

Fig 1 Factory Design Pattern Implementation

Here IElectronicToy is an interface with two functions namely play and stop. It represents a contract that each electronic toy should implement. The contract is dictate by two methods play() and stop(). TeddyBear and Lion are two classes that implements IElectronicToy interface. By overriding play() and stop() methods. TeddyBear and Lion each have different implementation of play() and stop() methods. ToyFactory is a class with just one static method CreateToy(..). This method accepts ToyType enum and returns either TeddyBear or lion depending upon ToyType value casted as IEletronicToy. Client represents a external class that calls ToyFactory class's static method createToy and passes appropriate value of ToyType. It in turn gets a object of type IElectronicToy which internally could be reprinting TeddyBear or Lion.

Here is java code that implements above classes.

File : IElectronic.cs

```
using System;
namespace Patterns
{
```

```csharp
public interface IElectronicToy {

    void play();
    void stop();
}

}
```

File: TeddyBear.cs

```csharp
using System;

namespace Patterns
{
    public class TeddyBear : IElectronicToy
    {

        public void play() {
            Console.WriteLine("Grrrrrr....");
        }

        public void stop() {
            Console.WriteLine("stopped grrrrr......");
        }
    }
}
```

File: Lion.cs

```csharp
using System;

namespace Patterns
{
    public class Lion  : IElectronicToy {

        public void play() {
            Console.WriteLine("Roar");
        }

        public void stop() {
```

```csharp
            Console.WriteLine("stopped roaring");
        }
    }
}
```

File: ToyFactory.cs

```csharp
using System;

namespace Patterns
{
    public class ToyFactory
    {

        public static IElectronicToy CreateToy(ToyType toyType)
        {
            IElectronicToy toy = null;
            switch(toyType)
            {
            case ToyType.TeddyBear:
                toy = (IElectronicToy) new TeddyBear();
                break;
            case ToyType.Lion:
                toy = (IElectronicToy) new Lion();
                break;

            default:
                throw new Exception("Unknown toyType " + toyType) ;

            }
            return toy;
        }
    }
}
```

File: ToyType.cs

```csharp
using System;

namespace Patterns
```

```
{
    public enum ToyType {
        TeddyBear,
        Lion
    }

}
```

File: Client.cs

```
using System;

namespace Patterns
{
    class MainClass
    {
        public static void Main (string[] args)
        {
            try
            {
                IElectronicToy                    toy           =
ToyFactory.CreateToy(ToyType.TeddyBear);
                toy.play();
                toy.stop();
                toy = ToyFactory.CreateToy(ToyType.Lion);
                toy.play();
                toy.stop();
            }
            catch(Exception ex)
            {
                System.Console.WriteLine(ex.Message);
            }
        }
    }
}
```

Output:

Grrrrrr....
stopped grrrrr......
Roar
stopped roaring

Press any key to continue...

Benefits

Reuse. If I want to instantiate one class from a family of related classed in many places, factory class can be used everywhere I need, without having to instantiate individual classes.

Unit-Testability. I can write 2 tests for the factory, to make sure it returns the correct types on the correct conditions, then calling class only needs to be tested to see if it calls the factory and then the required methods on the returned class. It needs to know nothing about the implementation of the factory itself or the concrete classes.

Extensibility. When someone decides we need to add a new class say Tiger to this factory, none of the calling code, neither unit tests or implementation, ever needs to be told. We simply create a new class Tiger and extend our factory method. This follows principles Open-Closed Principle.

You can even create a new factory class and make them hot-swappable, if the situation requires it for example, if you want to be able to switch class Lion on and off, while testing. I have run into this situation rarely, but it was extremely useful.

CHAPTER TWO

Abstract Factory

Background

Abstract Factory design pattern is one level of abstraction higher than factory pattern. You can use this pattern when you need to return one object from several related families.

Note that unlike factory patten, it says several families here not just one family. Therein lies key to understand abstract factory pattern. So abstract factory returns one factory from one of several factories.

One classic example of abstract factory pattern is in drawing animation objects like monkey, mountains on a screen. There could be several type of drawing systems like 2D, 3D and 4D. Each of these drawing system is capable of drawing animation objects. You could be creating a movie scene with a monkey jumping on from one tree to another tree on a muir wood mountain. You could play this scene by getting a factory for 2D and then play entire scene in 2D. Or you could ask for for 3D factory and play entire scene in 3D. This pluggable mechanism is extremely useful to compare how same scenes will be rendered in 2D, 3D or 4D just by asking for a specified factory without changing anything else. 2D, 3D and 4D represents different types of drawing platform. Abstract factory pattern encapsulates platform dependencies and simplifies use. It also allows easy exchange of platforms.

Implementation

Abstract factory pattern has 2 levels of abstraction. These two levels can be best illustrated with drawing example cited above. The use case here is to create a scene with a monkey jumping on a swaying tree. We would like to have a really easy way to change the rendering scene to 3D or 2D platform. First level of abstraction is achieved by using IDrawingPlatform and having TwodDrawingFactory and ThreeDdrawingFactory implementing IDrawingPlatform. Second level of abstraction is achieved by having each drawingFactory their own implementation of monkey and tree. IMonkey and ITree represents interfaces. TwoDMonkey and ThreeDMonkey implement IMonkey. TwoDTree and ThreeDTree implement ITree.

Client interacts with drawingPlatformFactory by passing it drawingType (2D or 3D) and seeking desired drawing of monkey or Tree. DrawingPlatformFactory first internally creates TwodDrawingFactory or ThreedDrawingFactory depending on drawingType. Client can then use this drawingFactory to draw desired shape of monkey or tree. This relationship is explained in picture below.

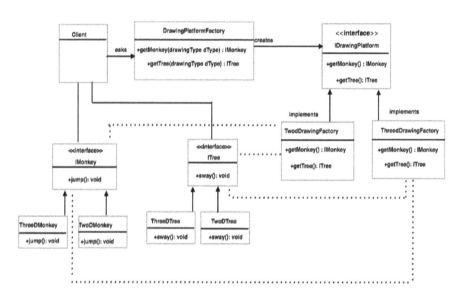

Fig 2 Abstract Design Pattern Implementation

Here is java code that implements above classes.

File: IMonkey.cs

using System;

namespace AbstractFactory
{
    public interface IMonkey {
        void jump();
    }
}

File: ITree.cs

```csharp
using System;

namespace AbstractFactory
{
    public interface ITree {
        void sway();
    }
}
```

File: IDrawingPlatform.cs

```csharp
using System;

namespace AbstractFactory
{
    public interface IDrawingPlatform {
        IMonkey getMonkey();
        ITree getTree();
    }
}
```

File: ThreeDMonkey.cs

```csharp
using System;

namespace AbstractFactory
{
    public class ThreeDMonkey : IMonkey {
        public void jump() {
            System.Console.WriteLine("This is 3d monkey jumping");
        }
    }
```

```csharp
}
```

File: TwoDMonkey.cs

```csharp
using System;

namespace AbstractFactory
{
    public class TwoDMonkey : IMonkey {

        public void jump() {
            System.Console.WriteLine("This is 2d monkey jumping");
        }
    }
}
```

File: ThreeDTree.cs

```csharp
using System;

namespace AbstractFactory
{
    public class ThreeDTree : ITree {
        public void sway() {
            System.Console.WriteLine("This is 3d tree swaying");
        }
    }
}
```

File: TwoDTree.cs

```csharp
using System;

namespace AbstractFactory
{
    public class TwoDTree : ITree {
        public void sway() {
            System.Console.WriteLine("This is 2d tree swaying");
        }
```

```
    }
}
```

File: TwoDDrawingFactory.cs

```
using System;

namespace AbstractFactory
{
    public class TwoDDrawingFactory : IDrawingPlatform{

        public IMonkey getMonkey() {
            return new TwoDMonkey();
        }

        public ITree getTree() {
            return new TwoDTree();
        }
    }
}
```

File: ThreedDrawingFactory.cs

```
using System;

namespace AbstractFactory
{
    public class ThreeDDrawingFactory : IDrawingPlatform{

        public IMonkey getMonkey() {
            return new ThreeDMonkey();
        }

        public ITree getTree() {
            return new ThreeDTree();
        }
    }
}
```

```csharp
    }
}
```

File: DrawingType.cs

```csharp
using System;

namespace AbstractFactory
{
    public enum DrawingType {
        TwoD,
        ThreeD
    }

}
```

File: DrawingPlatformFactory.cs

```csharp
using System;

namespace AbstractFactory
{
    public class DrawingPlatformFactory {

        public IMonkey getMonkey(DrawingType dType)
        {
            IMonkey theMonkey = null;
            switch(dType)
            {
            case DrawingType.TwoD:
                theMonkey = new TwoDMonkey();
                break;
            case DrawingType.ThreeD:
                theMonkey = new ThreeDMonkey();
                break;
            }

            return theMonkey;

        }
```

```csharp
public ITree getTree(DrawingType dType)
{
    ITree theTree = null;
    switch(dType)
    {
    case DrawingType.TwoD:
        theTree = new TwoDTree();
        break;
    case DrawingType.ThreeD:
        theTree = new ThreeDTree();
        break;
    }

    return theTree;

}

}
}
```

File : Client.cs

```csharp
using System;

namespace AbstractFactory
{
    public class Client {

        public static void Main(String[] args)
        {
            DrawingPlatformFactory drawingPlatform = new
DrawingPlatformFactory();
            IMonkey            theMonkey            =
drawingPlatform.getMonkey(DrawingType.TwoD);
            ITree theTree = drawingPlatform.getTree(DrawingType.TwoD);

            //Draw 2D Scene
            drawScene(theMonkey, theTree);

            theMonkey = drawingPlatform.getMonkey(DrawingType.ThreeD);
            theTree = drawingPlatform.getTree(DrawingType.ThreeD);
```

```
    //Draw 3D Scene
    drawScene(theMonkey, theTree);
}


private static void drawScene(IMonkey theMonkey, ITree theTree)
{
    theMonkey.jump();
    theTree.sway();
    }
  }
}
```

Output:
This is 2d monkey jumping
This is 2d tree swaying
This is 3d monkey jumping
This is 3d tree swaying

Benefits
Encapsulation: Abstract factory pattern isolates concrete classes completely from client. This allows interchange of product families freely.

Extensibility: Abstract Factory pattern is "factory of factories" and can be easily extended to accommodate more products, for example we can add another sub-class FourDDrawingFactory, FourDMonkey and FourDTree. Client code would require minimal changes.

CHAPTER THREE
Builder

Background

Builder design pattern is used to separate the construction of object from its representation. The same construction mechanism can be used to construct several different representations. Builder factor focuses on constructing object step by step. Consider an example of pizza shop. Customer can order for various types of pizzas like pepperoni pizza, supreme chicken pizza or veggie pizza. The steps for creating each pizza are same. The final outcome varies depending on what is done inside that step.

- Order pizza (Telephone/website/Go to the shop))
- Get a Pizza Base
- Add tomato sauce
- Add Cheese
- Add Toppings (Pepperoni/Veggie/Chicken)
- Bake The pizza
- Send the pizza to customer (Takeout or delivery)

Implementation

The use case here is to build a pizza based on customer specification. PizzaBuilder is an abstract class that dictates the steps to build pizza and also orchestrates the pizza making steps. VeggiePizzaBuilder, PizzaPepperoniBizzaBuilder and ChickenPizzaBuildera extends PizzaBuilderClass. The only method they override is addToppings() method. VeggiePizzaBuilder adds topics like tomato, green pepper and onions. PeopporoniPizzaBuilder adds pepperoni slices. ChickenPizzaBuilder adds grilled checkin toppings. Rest of the methods remain same for all three types of pizzas. Director class determines which PizzaBuilder class it should invoke based on PizzaType specification from customer. Client class represents customer who is placing the order. This relationship is explained in picture below. Note that '+' prefix in front of method denote public methods whereas '#' prefix denotes protected methods

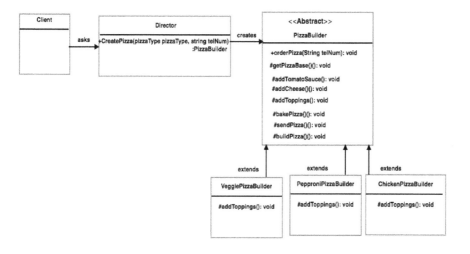

Fig 3 Builder Design Pattern Implementation

Here is java code that implements above classes.

File: PizzaType.cs

```csharp
using System;
namespace Builder
{
    public enum PizzaType {
        Veggie,
        Pepperoni,
        Chicken
    }
}
```

File: PizzaBuilder.cs

```csharp
using System;

namespace Builder
{
    public abstract class PizzaBuilder {

        protected String telNum = "";

        public void orderPizza(String telNum) {
            this.telNum = telNum;
            System.Console.WriteLine("Creating pizza for " + telNum);
            buildPizza();
        }
        protected void getPizzaBase() {
            System.Console.WriteLine("Getting pizza base");
        }
        protected void addTomatoSauce() {
            System.Console.WriteLine("Adding tomato sauce");
        }
        protected void addCheese() {
            System.Console.WriteLine("Adding cheese");
        }
        protected void bakePizza() {
            System.Console.WriteLine("baking pizza. Smells great");
        }
        protected void sendPizza() {
            System.Console.WriteLine("sending pizza to customer " +
this.telNum);
        }
        protected void buildPizza() {
```

```
            getPizzaBase();
            addTomatoSauce();
            addCheese();
            addToppings();
            bakePizza();
            sendPizza();
        }
        protected abstract void addToppings();
    }
}
```

File: VeggiePizzaBuilder.cs

```
using System;

namespace Builder
{
    public class VeggiePizzaBuilder : PizzaBuilder {

        protected override void addToppings() {
            System.Console.WriteLine("Adding onions, tomatoes and spinach") ;
        }
    }
}
```

File: PepporoniPizzaBuilder.cs

```
using System;

namespace Builder
{
    public class PepporoniPizzaBuilder : PizzaBuilder {

        protected override void addToppings() {
            System.Console.WriteLine("Adding Pepperoni") ;
```

```
        }
      }
}
```

File: ChickenPizzaBuilder.cs

```csharp
using System;

namespace Builder
{
    public class ChickenPizzaBuilder : PizzaBuilder {

        protected override void addToppings() {
            System.Console.WriteLine("Adding grilled chicken") ;
        }
    }

}
```

File: Director.cs

```csharp
using System;

namespace Builder
{
    public class Director {

        public static PizzaBuilder CreatePizza(PizzaType pizzaType, String telNum)
        {
            PizzaBuilder pizzaBuilder = null;

            switch(pizzaType)
            {

            case PizzaType.Veggie:
                pizzaBuilder = new VeggiePizzaBuilder();
                break;
```

```csharp
            case PizzaType.Pepperoni:
                pizzaBuilder = new PepporoniPizzaBuilder();
                break;
            case PizzaType.Chicken:
                pizzaBuilder = new ChickenPizzaBuilder();
                break;
            }
            pizzaBuilder.orderPizza(telNum);
            return pizzaBuilder;
        }
    }

}
```

File: Client.cs

```csharp
using System;

namespace Builder
{
    public class Client {

        public static void Main(String[] args) {
            System.Console.WriteLine("******* Ordering Pepperoni Pizza
*************");
            Director.CreatePizza(PizzaType.Pepperoni, "408-231-1234");
            System.Console.WriteLine("******* Ordering Veggie Pizza
*************");
            Director.CreatePizza(PizzaType.Veggie, "408-231-1244");
        }
    }
}
```

Output:
```
******* Ordering Pepperoni Pizza *************
Creating pizza for 408-231-1234
Getting pizza base
Adding tomato sauce
Adding cheese
Adding Pepperoni
baking pizza. Smells great
```

sending pizza to customer 408-231-1234
******* Ordering Veggie Pizza *************
Creating pizza for 408-231-1244
Getting pizza base
Adding tomato sauce
Adding cheese
Adding onions, tomatoes and spinach
baking pizza. Smells great
sending pizza to customer 408-231-1244

Benefits

Separation: Builder pattern lets you vary internal representation of the product it builds. It comes handy when you need to have lots of things to build an object. For example imagine a XML document object model. You have to create plenty of nodes and attributes to get your final object.

Extensibility: Builder pattern lets you reuse the same construction process for new objects.

CHAPTER FOUR
Prototype

Background

Prototype design pattern is used when creating an instance of a class is time intensive or complex. In such a case, ratter than creating new instances from scratch every time, you can create one instanced make copies of it and updating it as required. For instance if there are number of queries that needed to be made to get more information on an employee in database, a better approach would be to get the information of employee in a result set in memory only once, make copies of it for each query and then do the processing. This will prevent multiple round trips to database, thus reducing network overhead. Database connection happened to be one of limited and expensive resources in SaaS applications. Prototype patten offers help in reducing overhead by reducing object construction time and database round trips . These savings helps tremendously in scaling the SaaS application because resources like database connection, network connections are used more efficiently.

Prototype is unique among creational design pattern in that it does not require a class. It just needs an object. The key idea here is that an object can spawn other objects similar to itself. If you have one tree in computer game, you could create many trees just by cloning fret tree. All modern languages like Java, C# offers built in clone function at System.Object level that can be overridden by custom classes to achieve prototype functionality.

Implementation

The use case here is that client would like a construct a home. Home needs parts like doors and windows. Doors and windows of one home are similar in nature. They may vary by size.

DBContext is helper class that fetches default width and height from database. When home needs first door, we can create a basic door from scratch and keep it ready. First door is created using a constructor and it would call DbContext's getDefaultDoorHeight() and getDefaultDoorWidth() to get default width and height for door. It is time consuming call and requires 2 roundtrips to database.

When home needs another door, instead of creating from scratch, we can copy the data from first door and modify its properties as necessary. IClonable interface represents ability to copy an object. It just has clone() function. Any class that needs to implement copy functionality, they can override clone() function and provide their implementation of clone(). Door and Window class implement IClonable interface, thus provide ability to clone them. Client can call clone function on door and window object to create as any doors and windows as necessary for the home. When a door or window is cloned, we just make copy of existing object and then update as necessary. This cloning ability prevents expensive roundtrips to database.

This is depicted in picture below.

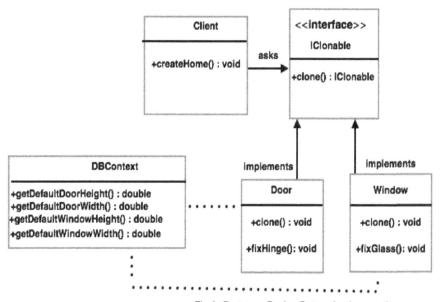

Fig 4 Prototype Design Pattern Implementation

Here is java code that implements above classes.

File: DBContext.cs

```csharp
using System;

namespace Prototype
{
    public class Window : IClonable {
```

```csharp
        public double glassSize = 10.0;
        public double width = 0.0;
        public double height = 0.0;

        public Window()
        {
            this.height = DBContext.getDefaultWindowHeight();
            this.width = DBContext.getDefaultWindowWidth();
        }


        public Object clone() {
            Window theWindow = new Window();
            theWindow.glassSize = this.glassSize;
            theWindow.width = this.width;
            theWindow.height = this.height;
            return theWindow;
        }

        public void fixGlass()
        {
            this.glassSize = 5.0;
            System.Console.WriteLine("Fixing glass to the window");
        }
    }

}
```

File: IClonable.cs

```csharp
using System;

namespace Prototype
{
    public class Window : IClonable {

        public double glassSize = 10.0;
        public double width = 0.0;
        public double height = 0.0;

        public Window()
```

```csharp
        {
                this.height = DBContext.getDefaultWindowHeight();
                this.width = DBContext.getDefaultWindowWidth();
        }


        public Object clone() {
                Window theWindow = new Window();
                theWindow.glassSize = this.glassSize;
                theWindow.width = this.width;
                theWindow.height = this.height;
                return theWindow;
        }

        public void fixGlass()
        {
                this.glassSize = 5.0;
                System.Console.WriteLine("Fixing glass to the window");
        }
    }

}
```

File: Window.cs
```csharp
using System;

namespace Prototype
{
    public class Window : IClonable {

        public double glassSize = 10.0;
        public double width = 0.0;
        public double height = 0.0;

        public Window()
        {
                this.height = DBContext.getDefaultWindowHeight();
                this.width = DBContext.getDefaultWindowWidth();
        }
```

```csharp
public Object clone() {
    Window theWindow = new Window();
    theWindow.glassSize = this.glassSize;
    theWindow.width = this.width;
    theWindow.height = this.height;
    return theWindow;
}

public void fixGlass()
{
    this.glassSize = 5.0;
    System.Console.WriteLine("Fixing glass to the window");
}

    }

}
```

File: Client.cs

```csharp
using System;

namespace Prototype
{
    public class Client
    {
        public static void Main(String[] args)
        {
            //Build a home with 2 doors and 4 windows

            //First door create from scratch
            Door door1 = new Door();

            //Build Second door by cloning first door
            Door door2 = (Door)door1.clone();

            door1.fixHinge();
            door2.fixHinge();
```

```csharp
//Build first window from scratch
Window window1 = new Window();

//Build 3 other windows by cloning first window
Window window2 = (Window)window1.clone();
Window window3 = (Window)window1.clone();
Window window4 = (Window)window1.clone();

window2.fixGlass();
window2.fixGlass();
window3.fixGlass();
window4.fixGlass();
        }
    }
}
```

Output:
Connecting to database...
Fetching default door height...
Connecting to database...
Fetching default door width...
Connecting to database...
Fetching default door height...
Connecting to database...
Fetching default door width...
Fixing hinge to the door
Fixing hinge to the door
Connecting to database...
Fetching default window height...
Connecting to database...
Fetching default window width...
Connecting to database...
Fetching default window height...
Connecting to database...
Fetching default window width...
Connecting to database...
Fetching default window height...
Connecting to database...
Fetching default window width...
Connecting to database...

Fetching default window height...
Connecting to database...
Fetching default window width...
Fixing glass to the window
Fixing glass to the window
Fixing glass to the window
Fixing glass to the window

Benefits

Scalability: Prototype pattern fast way to create new objects by cloning existing object which in turn improves efficiency of resource usage and improves scalability of overall system.

Simplicity and Consistency : Prototype patterns simplifies new object creation by enforcing cloning ability via IClonable interface. Using IClonable interface also makes closing behavior consistent across all classes.

CHAPTER FIVE

Singleton

Background

Singleton design pattern is used when as a designer of class, you need to control number of instances of your class that user can control . Specifically the number of instances that external consumer can create is restricted to one and only one. There are many use cases where restricting number of instances is obvious and safe choice. For instance the class that reads configuration information of application and is used as read only class should be singleton. Other examples of singleton classes are print spooler class,. Usually constructor of a Singleton class is made private. It just has a static method to access the only instance. The only instance serves as global point of access to the object.

Implementation

The use case here is that client would like access a configuration information of an application. This configuration information is stored in a text file in key value pairs.

Since same configuration information is needed in read only fashion everywhere, we just one instance of configuration reader. ConfigReader is a singleton class. Its constructor is made private so that client can not directly instantiate it. It has getInstance() method that Client can use to access the only instance it has. loadConfig() information is used for reading the information from text file during initialization part and keeps it in internal hash table. Once client contains instance of ConfigReader, it can get value of a configuration key by calling getValue() method by passing in value of key in question. getValue() function looks up hash table to get the value for specified key and returns it. The class diagram is depicted below.

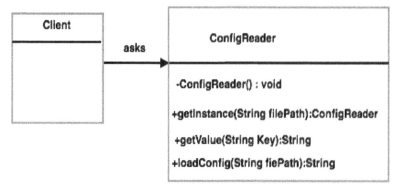

Fig 5 Singleton Design Pattern Implementation

Here is java code that implements above classes.

File: ConfigReader.cs

```
using System;
using System.Collections;
using System.IO;

namespace Singleton
{
    public class ConfigReader {
        private static ConfigReader _configReader = null;
        private Hashtable configTable = null;

        private ConfigReader() {
        }

        public static ConfigReader getInstance(String filePath) {
            if(_configReader == null) {
                _configReader = new ConfigReader();
                loadConfig(filePath);
            }

            return _configReader;
        }
```

```csharp
public static void loadConfig(String filePath)
{
    System.Console.WriteLine("loading config from file");
    string[] lines = File.ReadAllLines(filePath);
    _configReader.configTable = new Hashtable();

    foreach(string line in lines)
    {
        String key = line.Split('#')[0];
        String value = line.Split('#')[1];
        _configReader.configTable.Add(key, value);
    }

}

public String getValue(String key) {
    System.Console.WriteLine("getting config for key " + key);
    return (String)_configReader.configTable[key];
}
}


}


File: Client.cs

using System;
namespace Singleton
{

    public class Client {
        public Client() {
        }

        public static void Main(String[] args) {
            ConfigReader configReader = ConfigReader.getInstance("/Users/
ravindrasadaphule/config.txt");
            String                  dbConnectionString               =
configReader.getValue("DbConectionString");
            System.Console.WriteLine(dbConnectionString);
        }
    }
```

```
}
```

File: config.txt

DbConectionString#provider=oracle11;trusted_connection=yes
username#admin

Output:
loading config from file
getting config for key DbConectionString
provider=oracle11;trusted_connection=yes

Benefits

Low memory footprint: Singleton pattern restricts intense of a class to one. It prevents user from creating more than one instance and thus saves on memory.

Simplicity : Singleton pattern is deceptively simple. It is the pattern which completely contained in the same class and do not need any other auxiliary class.

CHAPTER SIX

Summary

Thank you very much for going through the entire book on creation design patterns. Here is brief summary of all creation al design patterns.

- **The Factory Pattern** is used to select and obtain an instance of a class from a number of similar classes based on data you provide to the factory.
- **The Abstract Factory Pattern** is used to obtain one of several related groups of classes. In some cases it returns a Factory for that group of classes.
- **The Builder Pattern** builds a number of objects to make a new object, based on the data with which it is presented.
- **The Prototype Pattern** clones an existing class rather than creating a new instance when creating new instances is more expensive.
- **The Singleton Pattern** is a pattern that ensures that there is one and only one instance of an object, and that it is possible to obtain global access to that one instance.